change

A working study of concepts found in the Edgar Cayce readings and the ancient Chinese oracle, I Ching.

A.R.E. PRESS ■ VIRGINIA BEACH ■ VIRGINIA

PREFACE

The project whose fruit you have before you began as an idealistic lark into two sources we had come to revere and study for some time. The real magnitude of our venture, and the audacity we were marked with by its attempt, became apparent to us upon beginning. To relate concepts found in an ancient Chinese oracular work to those present in the readings given by the contemporary psychic, Edgar Cayce, would require some knowledge-in-depth of both sources.

While the sixty-four hexagrams of the I Ching presented an orderly progression for exploration and comparison, the Edgar Cayce readings reached out into every direction of man's spiritual, mental and physical experience via numerous personal accounts. Some of the Cayce information we had available was categorized by broad subject headings, but a reading given on a physical, and apparently unrelated, problem might well contain information directly pertinent to the common spiritual thread we wanted to weave of the two sources.

We determined to begin with a basic understanding of the essence of each of the sixty-four hexagrams. I had previously done such a study, and the products of that study are the brief interpretations found herein. With these as a base, we immersed ourselves in various translations of the I Ching. When we were satisfied that we understood something of the concept in question, we began searching, page by page, for comparable points of view in the Edgar Cayce readings.

What we have done here should in no way be considered an attempt at a new translation of the I Ching. Rather, our only hope is that this small book may be useful to other students of The Way who are committed to what must ultimately be the single purpose of all men: to find oneness with God's purpose.

August, 1970
San Mateo, California

INTRODUCTION

All of the prominent spiritual movements share a common view regarding the successful realization of a spiritual ideal: ego must be translated into dedication to that ideal. True spiritual growth — the internal restructuring of the self — can take place no other way. The goal of the spiritually-directed individual, as we have earlier said, must be to find oneness with his God's purpose. The straightforward advice to "let go and let God" carries all the wisdom which the Seeker-on-The-Way must ultimately marry forever.

That there exists within each of us an area of rapport with all else, forward to eternity, backward to creation, the authors accept as basic. Within the silence of each man is a point of long-traveled light in which are held the knowings-beyond-time. Through his history, man has sought conscious identification with this God-within in his trials to make his steps coincide with the movements of God's great tides.

The intent of the I Ching is to assist the seeker in unifying himself with the God-perspective within him, so that the situation before him can be understood in terms of Cosmic Flow. Specifically: so that the Truth of that moment, for that individual, may become apparent to him.

The premise basic to the formation of the hexagrams — the six-line figures — is that what we see as a world of apparently disconnected events is actually one of continuous flow. What we perceive as an "event" is only the culminatory point-in-time of a series of infinitesimal movements toward that moment of perception.

Creation is constant: seeds are ever-bursting, the unseen is becoming visible, the visible coming to flower, wilting and passing beyond our perception once more. Consequently, since this moment is a product of events which subtly led to it, so *future* events should, given the essential focus and understanding, be visible in what is *presently* perceived.

Symbols for relationships both internal and external, symbols that the mind's center would use in analyzing and understanding, were established by the holy sages of ancient China. There was a hierarchy set up within the six lines of each of the sixty-four hexagrams which described a life-situation, conceptually if not

ii

actually. The circumstances thus depicted called forth certain potential consequences, and certain possibilities for internal and external growth in the ebb and flow of Cosmic cycles.

The I Ching also provides a model, a sage or superior man, whose action in the given circumstances one is encouraged to emulate. This man, in Western terms an obvious manifestation of the Christ Consciousness, is the consummate sage. He has achieved the goal of moving with the flow of God's law, of "letting go and letting God".

In his book, *Edgar Cayce on Religion and Psychic Experience,* Harmon H. Bro writes:

"In approaching patience as a religious question, the Cayce source appeared to be taking up the old religious question of how to correlate 'man's time' and 'God's time', how to recognize the *kairos,* or moment of readiness in one's affairs, when the personal and the trans-personal meet. It was the question of the Kingdom of God, always here and always coming — how to stand in its shadow and face the future. It was the question of 'storming the Kingdom' about which the prophets of Israel warned, as has the modern philosopher, Martin Buber: Each person must find the line which defines the difference between his readiness to act and his willful seizure of affairs. It was a question similar to those in Chinese discussions of the silent way of the Tao, similar to the encouragement of the Hindu *Bhagavad-Gita* that man could find a way to act without 'attachment to the fruits' of the action, and like the question of living faith in Muslim references to the 'will of Allah'."

The task the composers of the I Ching set themselves was to provide mankind with a means of understanding when "God's time" had arrived. They knew what Jesus later tells his followers, in saying that the Kingdom of God is within each of us. They were no strangers to meditation and contemplation, and they knew that each man would find his way if he could be brought to look in the right direction: inside, to the God-center.

He who, with humility and sincerity, consults the I Ching, sets up the climate requisite to God-communication. He commits himself to a spiritual direction with deliberateness and devotion. As in meditation, he establishes the necessary attitude of trusting receptivity. By these acts, and by the tossing of the

iii

coins, he sweeps aside the primary hindrance to his spiritual progress: the driving ego of his conscious self. What is obtained in response, therefore, comes through a context of unconscious selection.

We will not spend words in discussing the appropriateness of responses seen by us over the years; rather we will simply say that *all* were appropriate to the seeker's need. Many responses have been devastating in pinpointing the true question being asked.

We *will* put forth that the work, in the majority of cases, *begins* upon obtaining the oracular response. Never are the answers superficial, or obvious. They require an extension of the receptive and inquiring attitude preliminary to the consultation. In the manner of a great teacher, the faithful purpose of the ancients turns the book's inquisitor upon himself, so that the sought-after decision is finally found in the brightening circles of his own awareness.

Those readers interested in further investigating the I Ching might refer to the following:

The I Ching; Richard Wilhelm translation
The Text of Yi King; Z.D. Sung
I Ching; James Legg translation
The Nature of the I Ching; Charles Ponce

THE CONSULTING PROCESS

The easiest method to use in consulting the Book of Changes, and an entirely satisfactory one, is through the use of three coins. Although it lends color to the ritual to use Chinese coins (those with the square hole in the center), the sole recommendation we would make is that the coins be like-sized, to facilitate handling. Any coins upon which one can distinguish a "head" side and a "tail" side will do.

In setting the stage for the proper use of this ancient process, it should be remembered that the coins are representative of the yielding up of the "outer" self to the "inner". They are the instruments of commitment to a choice made by a level of self which knows The Truth for your needs will become evident through your own experience.

Approach the Oracle with the same reverent attitude of mind which precedes meditation or prayer. Mental clarity will assist both the consulting process and the analysis of the response received. Be totally aware of the direction you are consciously taking. There is much to be gained from such focused dedication.

The process is as follows:

First, be sure that you have a good grasp of your question. Writing it down is a good idea, as it will help you to keep the question in focus as you go along. You'll need paper and a pencil to build your hexagram.

Take up the three coins and, with the question rooted in your mind, shake the coins vigorously and let them fall. Reading Heads as a value of *three* and Tails as *two,* total the coins.

An even answer (six or eight) produces a broken line; an odd answer (seven or nine) produces a solid line.

The coins should be thus thrown six times, which will give your six-line response. The hexagram is built from the bottom up, as in the following example:

Throw No.	Result	Value	Line Produced
6	H-T-T	7	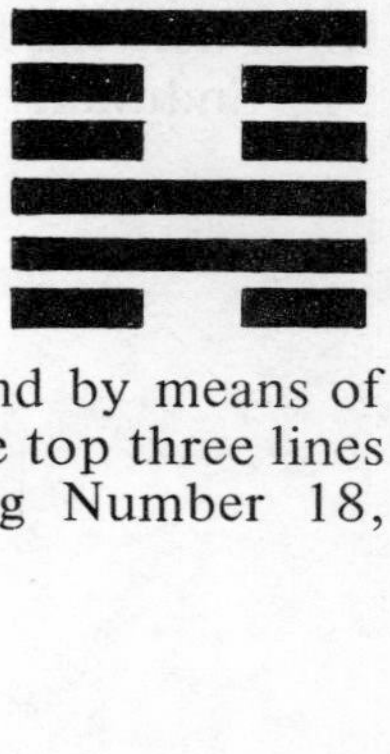 ▅▅▅▅▅
5	H-H-T	8	▅▅ ▅▅
4	T-T-T	6	▅▅ ▅▅
3	T-T-H	7	▅▅▅▅▅
2	H-H-H	9	▅▅▅▅▅
1	H-T-H	8	▅▅ ▅▅

The text of the hexagram given above is found by means of the chart provided in the back of the book. The top three lines are matched to the bottom three, indicating Number 18, Rejuvenation.

v

THE SIXTY-FOUR HEXAGRAMS

1 Creativity

Creativity is a constant —
flowing through our lives and our
world; the very essence of all things.
It is one moment built upon its
predecessor, the continuous flow
of existence. From this, the cosmic
example, one must model his inner self,
aspiring to consistency in his moments
of cosmic unity. It is in this construct
of persistent contact and identification
with the ceaseless power of heaven that
the goal is realized.

The soul of each individual is a portion then of the Whole, WITH the birthright of Creative Forces to become a co-creator with the Father, a co-laborer with Him. As that birthright is then manifested, growth ensues. If it is made selfish, retardments must be the result.

And Oh that all would realize, come to the consciousness, that what we are — in any given experience, or time — is the combined results of what we have done about the ideals that we have set!

We find — as given from the beginning, each may attain to that whereunto it has set and does set itself, according to the consciousness of the indwelling of the Creative Forces within.

For He has promised to meet and to be with those who call, and who do His biddings, and keep His commandments. And if He comes and abides with thee, what would be the limitations? There are none, from the spiritual angle. And it is spirit — in self, in the Creative Forces — that will and does direct. 1549-1

2 Receptivity

If one is to be in touch with
the cosmic flow, he must develop a consciousness that will permit communication. Through the wide gate of his
spirit's awareness, the sage receives the
earth-intended force and humbly puts it
to use for all men. Through this attitude
of serving, he builds cooperation so that
men may learn to work together in the
shaping of their destinies.

And the centers becoming attuned — to the vibration of the
bodily force — these give a vision of that which may be to the
entity an outlet for self-expressions, in the beauties and
harmonies and activities that become — in their last analysis —
just being p tient, longsuffering, gentle, kind. THESE are the
fruits of th spirit of truth; just as hates, malice and the like
become — in their growths — those destructive forces in
creating, ı making for those things that are as but tares,
confusions, dissensions in the experiences of an entity.   987-4

This ye may ask day by day: LORD, SHOW THOU ME THE
WAY. LET ME NOT IN MIND, IN PURPOSE, IN INTENT,
DICTATE TO ANY: BUT THOU, O GOD, DIRECT THE
WAYS, THE PURPOSES.

In that attitude ye may create about thy loved ones, thy
friends, thy brethren, that sureness in Him that may bring
about the NEEDS for that life, that experience of thy son in
the vineyard of the Lord.   602-7

3 PROPER BEGINNINGS

It is the time to begin. The strength required to begin, however, is not yet equal to the powerful external forces. To begin alone would be disastrous. Assistance is required, and to attract this help one must show receptivity, even humility. Force, arrogance, independent action bring ruin. In this sweeping aside of the ego, this recognition of one's weakness, lies the perspective, the consciousness required to transform chaos into the beginnings of the path.

The environs then — in the earth, in any given experience, — are those things that make for the emotional body in that experience.

That which is innate, or that which finds expression when the individual soul turns to the Creative Force or God within, arises from the soul's experience in those environs about the earth.   852-12

Q: Please give advice that would help in those times when there is the beginning of kundalini . . .

A: Surround self with that consciousness of the Christ-Spirit; this by the affirmation of "Let self be surrounded with the Christ-Consciousness, and the DIRECTION be through those activities in the body-force itself."

Do not seek the lower influences, but the Christ-Consciousness.
2072-11

4 Learning Faith

Beginnings are fraught with doubts and indecision. One has not the knowledge to confidently set out, and there is the tendency to question the reality of the path, and to point to the confusion pressing in from every side. It is the internal framework that needs ordering and cohesiveness, not the external. What is called for is a looking-inward to build one's faith and character.

For, when the will to do is ever present and not faltered by doubts and fears that may arise in the experience of all, then does it build, then does it attract that which builds and builds and is the constructive force in the experience of all.   416-2

And when this influence, this growing self becomes such, or so self centered, as to lose sight of that desire, purpose, aim to be TO the glory of its source, and seeks rather FOR self, then it errs in its application of the influences within its abilities for the application of mind within its own experience.   1947-3

Nothing prevents (soul or spiritual development) only self. Keep self and the shadow away. Turn thy face to the light and the shadows fall behind.   987-4

5 Learning Patience

A belief in life includes an acceptance of life's cyclical nature. To persist when passivity is called for exhibits a lack of faith. Here is a time to wait, not impatiently, not anxious to continue on one's way, but with the joyful knowledge that *this* is the way. This inner certainty is true courage, which will eventually transcend any obstacle.

Because of discouragements and because of failures, and because of heartaches, and because of those things that make men afraid, will ye turn thy back upon the opportunity before thee now?

Then what is the real problem?

Hold fast to that which ye purpose in thy heart, — that there WILL be the opportunity for those that are — through their own shortcomings — losing, — or have lost sight of their relationships.   165-26

So, it is to learn, then, that which is as a portion of life — as would be noted that was not named as to what Life is in a manifested form, in this experience — the lesson of patience — PATIENCE!

Hence the more oft there is the humbling of the spirit that there may be the better hold, a better understanding gained.

1402-1

6 Evaluating Strife

Because the way is long and confusing at times, one may easily set off in a wrong direction with the sincerest of intentions. Certainly, it is well to take care in preparation for the journey. If it becomes apparent that the way chosen is beset with conflict, it is well to pause and consider the motivations that brought one to this uneasy place. In this the higher self should be consulted. To insist on continuing, when continuation is questionable, is to invite disaster.

This should ever be considered: . . . If one in error practices that error, the error becomes more and more prominent in the activity of that soul; whether in thought, in faith or in practice.

For each soul must apply — especially spiritual, but also mental truths in its own experience.　416-2

Let the body-mind continue in the attitude of seeking for SPIRITUAL awakening. Know that each experience in this material plane is — if used in a constructive manner — FOR SOUL DEVELOPMENT!　1445-1

These as given are not merely sayings; they answer to that which has been and is thy turmoil in the present. Look WITHIN! For if there is trouble in thy mind, in thy body, in thy spirit or purpose, or mind; sin lieth at that door.　1537-1

When crisis threatens, what is called for is self-organization, inner strength and constancy in what is right. To proceed without regard for morality is always wrong. One is increased by one's generous behavior toward others, both in receiving their support, and in the cosmic's positive reaction to this humility.

In the spirit is strength. Give that strength an opportunity of manifesting itself in thine life; as it is manifested in the lives of those whom the entity contacts. Make thine life beautiful, and it becomes more worthwhile. 2096-1

This entity may play upon the emotions of others, using the emotions as stumbling-blocks or it may use them as stepping-stones. It may use opportunities to raise others to the point of anxiety or to the point where they would spend their souls for the entity; using the emotions as buildings or as serpents or scorpions. It may love very deeply, either for the universal consciousness or for the gratifying only self or the physical emotions.

Again the entity may express each of the emotions in their counterpart, — as patience, longsuffering, brotherly love, kindness, gentleness . . . [The entity] can look on others and smile and love to the extent of being willing to give all for the cause or purpose.

These are abilities latent and manifested in this entity. Use them, do not abuse them . . . Use them to the glory of thy ideal, and let that ideal be set in that way of the Cross. 3637-1

8 Cooperation

Often the best way to meet danger is by joining with others. As in the situation in hexagram 3, this admission of need pushes aside the ego, permitting adequate receptivity. It is well to listen to the inner self when one is threatened. One should also be ever mindful of his basic unity with his fellows, allowing them to help him, for the sharing of responsibilities fosters brotherhood.

In thy service to those thou would entertain — something is given out that arouses helpful hopefulness in the experience of the individual or the group or the masses that ye would entertain.

For whether ye preach a sermon, or whether ye entertain in those manners as befitting to the activities of the group, let it be done with an eye-singleness of *service,* of *joy,* of helpfulness to thy fellow man.

Let thy desires towards them be that ye would bring joy, hope and gladness in their hearts, their minds.

And let each and every program contain something of a *spiritual* awakening; not only for self, but as ye give, as ye do unto thy fellow man, ye are doing unto the God in thyself.

887-3

9 humble strength

Here is not a time for action, except on a limited basis. One may possess the strength, but the conditions are not favorable. The cycle of preparation is not yet complete. The inner man should be strong, but the outer man should manifest gentleness. Any progress must be subtly achieved.

Study self. Be humble, but not timid. Be positive, but not in that determination of rule or ruin. But rather in that as was given by Jesus — mercy, justice, patience, love, long-suffering, brotherly kindness, and forgetting those things that easily beset one in grudges or hatreds or hard feelings — but rather study others. DO NOT let things RULE, but give them — as to self, as to others — their proper sphere, their proper place, in the experience of others. 1402-1

Open the door for those that cry aloud for a knowledge that God is within the reach of those that will put their hand to DOING; just being kind — not a great deed as men count greatness, but just being gentle and patient and loving even with those that would despitefully use thee. For the beauties of the Lord are with those that seek to know and *witness* for Him among men. 1436-1

10 Right Conduct

If one proceeds respectfully when one is near danger, behaving decorously, achievement is possible. Here is a time for discriminating between things, classifying most and least importants, and giving attention to duty accordingly. Those around you will respond to your well-ordered behavior positively.

Through your efforts alone little may be done, yet through that which you and your consciousness are able to direct, much will be accomplished. As the necessary conditions arise, that which is best will be given you. 900-345

Not in selfishness, not in grudge, not in wrath; not in *any* of those things that make for the separation of the I AM from the Creative Forces, or Energy, or God. But the simpleness, the gentleness, the humbleness, the faithfulness, the long-suffering, *patience!* These be the attributes and those things which the soul takes cognizance of in its walks and activities before men. 518-2

11 Balance

Here conditions are almost in accord with positive action; harmony waxes. Still, it is well not to lean too far in any direction, but rather to strive to achieve a balance in one's life, between the spiritual and physical. By examining these two worlds separately, one can better understand and amplify their gifts to man.

There are some conditions of which the body needs to be wary, from the physical, mental and spiritual aspects. For the soul, spirit and physical must ever remember that the material body is but the temple through which the mental forces, with the will, builds to the I AM that must ever live. And without the perfectly balanced forces the best can not be given nor manifested . . .   2801-1

For with each and every force applied in the physical there must be corresponding force applied in the subliminal or spiritual force in the body.   140-1

12 Exercising faith

The cooperative conjunction of the spiritual and physical has passed, and the balance of conditions tips toward the unfavorable. If one has developed an inner focus through which to maintain the positive perspective, one slides through the difficulties. One should quietly maintain one's self-esteem, eschewing temptation and the pressing negative influences.

Then put on the whole armor. Look within self first. Clear that doubt of thy connection with that divine source, — that WITH which ye may conquer ALL — and WITHOUT which even all the fame, all the fortune of age would not bring that ye have purposed to do, into the experience of even ONE soul. But whom the Lord would exalt. He first brings low that they may know the strength is of the Lord and not in hosts but the still small voice that beareth witness with thy soul, thy spirit, — that ye walk that straight and narrow way that leadeth to understanding. And in saving those of thy own shortcomings, ye find ye have been lifted up.   165-26

When circumstances, as here, require that many unite to achieve a goal, what is needed is that their separate drives be discarded in favor of an organized, collective effort. The quality of open sincerity helps to remove the walls of distrust that often divide men. The goal, and the means of getting to it, should be clearly defined for all concerned.

For in the manifestation of spirit and mind and matter, — like begets like — if the entity shows itself friendly, there will be friends — if the entity manifests itself in those things pertaining to a universal consciousness, that it is the good for all rather than the individual or individual group. Courting favor with others, that there may be favor shown self is not so good — unless it is prompted by a universal desire to be of help in many directions.   3226-1

14 Use of Power

When conditions for progressive action are at their optimum, there is a responsibility to use the increased powers reverently, to curb evil and foster good. Power used in the name of good reaps great benefit for the user, bringing him into a balance with the cosmic supplier, and giving him a truer perspective as to the nature and origin of power.

And if the entity learned eventually in that experience, so will it in this: All such must emanate from the spiritual, for a spiritual purpose and not the use or abuse of spiritual forces for material gains. 2144

When there is delegated power to a body that has separated itself from the spirit (or coming from the unseen into the seen, or from the unconscious into the physical consciousness, or from God's other door — or opening from the infinite to the finite), then the activity is life; with the will of the source of that which has come into being. As to what it does with or about its associations of itself to the source of its activity, as to how far it may go afield, depends upon how high it has attained in its ability to throw off both negative and positive forces. Hence, we say, "The higher he flies the harder the fall." It's true! Then, that which has been separated into the influence to become a body, whether celestial, terrestrial, or plain clay manifested into activity as man, becomes good or bad. The results to the body so acting are dependent and independent (interbetween, see) upon what he does with the knowledge of — or that source of — activity. 262-52

Whatever the conditions, one must take great care to maintain an equilibrium in one's thoughts and activities, since an overbalance — giving too great or too little an emphasis to an aspect of experience — will impede one's progress toward the goal. Keeping an even perspective toward all things is a central key to completion of the journey.

For all (elements) have their relation one to another in each soul. FOR OF THE MENTAL THE SOUL FEEDS.

The body must be well-rounded in physical and mental attributes, that the soul may develop and that the spiritual will remain with the entity as the guiding force in the correct and upright channels.   900-8

For with each and every force applied in the physical there must be corresponding force applied in the subliminal or spiritual force in the body.

Without this entity having these forces coordinated, nothing becomes a whole to this body.   140-1

Keep the spiritual and mental in control of the physical, that the oneness of the universal force and love — found in Him — may manifest in a material way in the physical body.   294-10

16 Rededication

As in 14, conditions bode well, but there is the danger of carelessness due to overconfidence. It behooves one to pause and reestablish oneself spiritually, even dedicating oneself to the will of the cosmic. In this way one can lessen the possibility of directional error and also create the personal aura necessary in attracting cooperation from others.

Ye are allowing much of the material things to become stumbling-blocks to thy spiritual and thy soul development . . .

There must be in the heart, in the mind, in the soul of every entity — that which is its ideal, its God, its trust, its hope.

And they that trust in themselves alone are not wise!

Rather know WHO is the author of thy wisdom. WHO is the keeper of thy hopes? In WHOM have ye believed?   1599-1

For knowledge is power, and all force, all power, emanates from the one source.   262-97

The activity of an entity (soul-body-mind) as a unit, in whatever sphere or experience or consciousness it may function, is as the thread of life that connects with that which is to be opened when those experiences are to be made as one with that Universal Consciousness.   619-5

Although one must take care whom, or what, one elects to follow, service to another's path will bring understanding found no other way. If one is ever to lead, one must know what it is to follow. As in all life experiences, sincerity of purpose and thoughtful observation are requisites to success. It is important to keep the self prepared, through rest and renewing meditation, to continue on the path.

Do not be afraid of giving self in a service, if the IDEAL is correct. If it is for selfish motives or for aggrandizement, or for obtaining a hold to be used in an underhanded manner — BEWARE. If it is that the glory of truth may be made manifest, SPEND IT ALL, whether self, mind, body, or the worldly means, — whether in labor or in the coin of the realm.   1957-1

For until ye are willing to LOSE thyself in service, ye may not indeed know that peace which He has promised to give all.   1599-1

Now, when there has been and is made the best possible effort that self may give to do that which is in keeping with His will (as is understood by self), leave the results in His hands; for whom the Lord quickeneth may be turned into those channels that may make for those associations which will give the channel for the better service to self, to others.

Make known the desires to channels, to those associations and connections that may be had. Then wait ye on Him. 243-15

18 Rejuvenation

Stagnation is an abnormal state in a context of constant creativity. It is the responsibility of one who possesses the perspective and the strength to motivate conditions out of lethargy into continued growth. Here again, it is well to meditate in preparation and as a staying force.

As to the attitude then, of self: How well do ye wish to be? How well are ye willing to cooperate, coordinate with the Divine influences which may work in and through thee by stimulating the centers which have been latent with nature's activities. For all of these forces must come from the One Source, and the applications are merely to stimulate the atoms of the body. For each cell is as a representative of a universe in itself. Then what would ye do with thy abilities?

As ye give to others, not hating them, to know more of the Universal Forces, so may ye have the more, for God is love. Do that and ye will bring bettered conditons for yourself. Work where you are. As was given to those who were called, "The ground upon which ye stand is holy." Begin where you are.

4021-1

True, there are pathological conditions that are disturbed with this body. But do the first thing first. There should be a decision within self, first, as to what you believe. And know it must begin with the spiritual purposes of life.

3174-1

Because one understands the cyclic nature of existence and that the tide will turn, one must use a propitious time to its best advantage. Channeling the waxing positive cosmic forces, one nourishes the minds and hearts of all those around him through instruction and example, thereby expressing the inexhaustibility of good.

As ye apply, as ye make use of that in hand, more is given thee. For, day unto day is sufficient, if use is made thereof; not to self, not to self alone. Not that self is not to be considered, but losing self in good is the better way to FIND self.

What is good? How is such defined in thy life of awakening to all the possibilities that exist in thy intake of life and its phases? To do good is to think constructively, to think creatively. What is creative, what is constructive, ye may ask? That which never hinders, which never makes for the bringing of any harm to others. 1206-13

20 Right teaching

To truly know a thing one must experience it. To understand other people one must come into contact with their lives and see their deepest needs. Then one can teach with true sympathy and what one has to give is well received.

As indicated, it is not by might, nor by some great deed (as the entity saw illustrated in that experience), nor by something that may be spoken of by others, but as He has given so oft, — it is here a little, there a little, — line upon line, precept upon precept; SOWING the fruits of the spirit, LEAVING the fruition of same to God. . .   1877-2

In mercy, in justice, in love then — deal thy abilities to thy associates and thy fellow man . . .   3637-1

Rather choose thou as he of old, — let others do as they may, but as for thee, serve thou the living God. Thus ye may constructively use that ability of spiritual attunement, which is the birthright of each soul; ye may use it as a helpful influence in thy experiences in the earth.   2475-1

21 Understanding the Law

Because few have the constant perspective of the sage, guide-lines are necessary for men, that they may understand that actions breed consequences. Experiencing these consequences is often the only way man truly learns where the path is not. One may help, in this regard by plainly outlining the law and the results of breaking it.

Most individuals in the present misinterpret karmic conditions. The development or destiny, as karmic influences, each soul entity should gain the proper concept of destiny. Destiny is within; it is of faith; or is as the gift of the Creative Forces. Karmic influence, is then, rebellious influence against destiny.   903-23

The entity puts a stress upon karma. Thus, as may be the experience, if ye live by law, you must judge by law. If ye live by faith, ye judge by faith . . . Viewed from the spirit, much of time and space in a material concept loses its relationship and becomes *now*. Hence those experiences which have brought distortions in the material plane are not merely because of karmic law, but the application of karmic law in the life of the individual entity.   2981-1

22 Genuineness

While it is a virtue to manifest one's life in a visibly creative and graceful manner, it must be remembered that artistry of performance is only the veneer. Acting out the correct move at the appropriate time will often see one through, but development of one's inner light must be undertaken if any meaningful growth is to take place.

So we have LOVE is LAW. LAW IS LOVE. GOD IS LOVE. LOVE IS GOD. In that we see the law manifested, not the law itself. Unto the individual, as we have given then, that gets the understanding of self, becomes a part of this. As is found, which come in one, so we have manifestations of the one-ness, of the all-ness in love. Now, if we, as individuals, upon the earth plane, have all of the other elementary forces that make to the bettering of life, and have not love we are as nothing — nothing. "Though one may have the gift of prophecy, so as to give great understanding, even of the graces in Hope, in Charity, in Faith, and has not the law of love in their heart, soul, mind and though they give their body to give itself for manifesting even these graces, and has not love — they are nothing." In many, many ways may the manifestations of the law of love be shown, but without the greater love, even as the Father giveth, even as the soul giveth, there is no understanding, and no compliance of the forces that make our later law to this, of effect. 3744-42

During a period of adversity, although one must arrest his forward progress it is possible to at least maintain the position already attained. By the generous giving to those who are less fortunate, one fulfills the responsibility of position and thereby does not lose ground.

Or it comes to this: He that gives the kind word, even coals of fire are heaped upon the soul, shall be recompensed in saving not only self and the growth of self's own soul, but many another . . .

Faint not and know He is able to bear thee up, lest thou — in thine distress — bring even a greater sorrow in thine experience.

290-1

Think of that which has been indicated, that as ye measure to others it will be measured to you!

In thy associations and dealings with thy fellow man, manifest that rule (and not by feelings alone, to be sure), that as ye would that men would consider thee if thy positions were reversed, so act toward thy fellow man.

1901-1

24 Attunement

Here is a period to avoid ill-timed movement, while swelling one's awareness of the ebb and flow of all things. The time for action approaches; the inner resources are being recharged by the cosmic swing toward rebirth. One must be receptive and patient, not outgoing.

With the periods set aside for meditation — don't hurry yourself, don't be anxious, but closing the self, the conscious mind to anxieties from without — enter within thine own inner temple. There let the voice, the feeling, direct; yea, let the spirit of the purpose of self be free in its direction to self.

Attune yourself almost in the same manner as you tune the violin for harmony. For when the body-mind and the soul-mind is attuned to the infinite, there will be brought harmony to the mind and those centers from which impulse arises will aid in the directing of the individual entity to become more sensitive and the material things about the entity may be the better enjoyed . . .   1861-18

25 purity of purpose

 Man contrives to be many things that he is not, in order to build the ego's world. To manifest one's life artificially can only lead to ruin. To be oneself is to join nature's harmony, whereby one can, by one's very purity of being, give inspiration to others.

In analyzing the body-mind, also those purposes and ideals which have been and may be the ideals of this entity; One, as this entity, learns by experience that there are things in which the entity may apply itself and there are things and conditions in which the entity may not apply itself. Yet the Lord thy God is one. Thus these few, simple rules may apply in the experiences of this entity:

First, ye must believe that God is. Thus ye may believe that He is a rewarder of those who diligently seek Him, in opening, in interpreting the experiences of the entity in this life to a more perfect understanding. Know there is the straight and narrow way. They who seek same may find Him, but there must be the application of self towards the ideals presented through those very impulses which brought this to bear in thy experience. Thus may it be summed up, as ye would that others should do to you, do ye even so to them. This is the law and the prophets.

3051-7

26 Setting forth

One must leave the sanctuary of his home and put to work the principles he espouses intellectually, or his life has little meaning. It strengthens one's faith to leave the securities of a familiar environment and face the world's tests. Preparation for such forays should include inspirational teachings of those who have preceded, as this will build both humility and confidence.

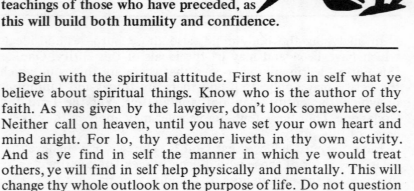

Begin with the spiritual attitude. First know in self what ye believe about spiritual things. Know who is the author of thy faith. As was given by the lawgiver, don't look somewhere else. Neither call on heaven, until you have set your own heart and mind aright. For lo, thy redeemer liveth in thy own activity. And as ye find in self the manner in which ye would treat others, ye will find in self help physically and mentally. This will change thy whole outlook on the purpose of life. Do not question as to what others will say or do but find in thy self how and why God, in His wisdom and mercy, has given thee the opportunity — for thyself, . . . to be a witness for Him, thy God in the earth.   3359-1

Knowledge without works is sin.   815-7, A-3

27 true nourishment

True nourishment is that which furthers one's progress on the path. That which brings growth to man is what he should seek; what he ingests, be it food or thought, should not cause deviation in his development. It follows that a pursuit which impedes one's progress should be shunned.

In this attitude should the body ever keep self, in that at-onement, that attunement, so that those material things — as become manifestations of that thought in the mental body — are directed by that same spiritual force as makes for continued creative energy, and constructive in its every action. For that builded, that held in the mental image of one, becomes the conditions — when they (that held) become material, or crystallized into material things. 589-1

Study to show thyself approved unto Him, rightly divining the words of truth, keeping self unspotted from the world, avoiding the appearance of evil, for as is given, those who would seek God must believe that He IS, and a rewarder of those who would seek Him. That is, that the Creator has that oneness with the individual to make that oneness with Him. As is given in the conditions as manifest through those who would seek the oneness with God, for only those who have approached sufficient to make the mind of the physical, the mind of the soul, the mind of the spiritual, one with Him, may understand or gather that necessary to approach that understanding. 900-21, A-5

28 True Courage

When conditions demand that some new directional move be made, the sage is one who has the courage to begin, even though such movement would seem to be contrary to majority opinion. One should proceed, as always, with humility, but firm in his faith that cosmic winds blow at his back.

And the abilities are here to accomplish whatever the entity would choose to set its mind to, so long as the entity trusts not in the might of self, but in His grace, His power, His might. Be mindful ever of that, in thy understanding in thy own wisdom, much may be accomplished but be rather thou the channel through which He, God, The Father, may manifest His power — in whatever may be the chosen activity of the entity.   3183-1

The way is long and difficult. Again and again one's faith and strength are pushed to the limit. If one is to reach the goal, he must maintain consistency, both in thought and deed. He must use his contact with his spiritual source as one uses a signal-beacon, to guide him home. It is through living one's beliefs, internally and externally, that the difficulties are transcended and success won.

Use those conditions as come into the experience of the life as stepping stones for *better* things, not allowing *them* to overcome and to subdue the abilities! 279-1

For, God hath not purposed or willed that any soul should perish, but purgeth everyone by illness, by prosperity, by hardships, by those things needed, in order (for the individual) to meet self. But in Him, by faith and works, are ye made every whit whole. 3395-2

But no urge, no karmic force even, surpasses the *will* of the entity in any given experience or choice to be made. 1554-2

30 living truth

If one's existence is to be meaningful, if one's words are to have weight,
he must *be* an extension of the truths
which have nourished mankind through the
ages. It is those things to which a man
adheres that he becomes, and manifests, so
he must choose his philosophical direction
with care. It is enough to perpetuate the
existing brightness of truth — one need
not be assertive in some new way.

As ye live those precepts that are His, — that is, ye shall love
the Father as thyself, with all thy heart, with all thy mind,
with all thy body, thy neighbor as thyself — ye manifest His
glory . . .

In the application of those tenets, those principles, in
dealing with others, they may be manifested in the fruit of the
spirit, — patience, longsuffering, gentleness, kindness, brotherly
love. These are manifestations of the spirit of that Christ. In
self they may grow, as is the ability in self to come to that
knowledge, that awakening of His promises abiding ever in thee.
And such administrations of love may bring healing, in body,
in mind, to others.   2441-4

Here the conditions are auspicious for progress and achievement. Yet misfortune can result from being assertive unless one ensures the co-operation of his fellows. The sage is one who is always willing to listen to others' points of view. It is through this openness that he fosters a sense of harmony, and gains the support of those around him.

Ever, EVER, the fruits of the spirit in their awareness: Long-suffering, brotherly love, patience, kindness, gentleness, HOPE and faith! If ye, in thy activities in any manner with thy fellow man, destroy these in the minds, in the hearts of thy fellow man, ye are not only slipping but ye have taken hold on the path of destruction. Then so live, so act, so THINK that others SEEING thy good works, thy hopes that ye bring, thy faith that ye manifest, thy patience that ye show may ALSO glorify Him.

For that cause, for that purpose ye entered into materiality in the present. 826-11

32 Endurance

It is the nature of the world that constant adjustment be made to external conditions. The way of man's progress is varied, taking him through a myriad of experiences. Through it all, one should maintain an inner direction which keeps him from deviating from the path. It is this internal direction which manifests itself to the world as wisdom and light.

Through patience and endurance does the crown of joy, happiness, as the peace of His presence, give those blessings that are from His throne. His presence, with peace, is the promise of those who with patience endure the crosses, that are set before thee day by day.

Keep the faith, and in patience know in what thy faith is placed; for it is as the crucible and the test of all attributes as related to the forces in the earth to the Father in glory.

In patience does the knowledge of the peace and understanding of His presence come. An active force, not a passive one. Necessary that patience be exercised that ye know the hope, the faith, the knowledge, the understanding of His ways in the earth.

Watch, that ye be not overcome. Watch and pray, for as the Father giveth so does the understanding come as to what may be accomplished in the efforts of the self in relationships to others; and ye are the light-bearers for Him.   262-26

33 Combating Negativity

When inferior forces are waxing, one only exhausts himself in attempting to subdue them head-on. It is better to yield ground and keep as free from contact with the on-moving evil as is possible. This is a time for introspection and patience, for developing understanding and tolerance of others' perspectives.

But to prevent physical harm, mental harm, — attune self in body, in mind with that influence by which the entity seeks to be directed; not haphazardly, not by chance, — but as of old — choose thou this day WHOM ye will serve; the living God within thee, by thee, through thee? or those influences of knowledge without wisdom, that would enslave or enpower thee with the material things which only gratify for the moment?

2475-1

Then only in LOVING indifference may the conditions be met. What, ye say, is loving indifference? Acting as if it had not been, save disregarding — as if they were NOT.

Not animosity, for this only breeds strife. Not anger, for this will only produce mentally and physically the disturbances that become physical reactions that prevent meeting every phase of the experience; whether in the good, the hope, the help ye mete to others, or in keeping self unspotted from the *cares* of the world.

1402-2

34 Resisting Temptation

In a time of great personal power it especially behooves one to bear his ideals in mind. There is the temptation to go beyond the limits of what is proper, when the cosmic flow is with one's every movement. The sage is one who does not forget his responsibility to the good, no matter how great his power waxes.

Ye are in the position, ye have been especially endowed with the faculties and abilities to be of a service to thy fellow man. Will ye do so that thine own ego may be satisfied; that ye may enjoy the pleasures of thine own appetites for a season; using thy obligations, using thy opportunities as an excuse that ye may gratify thine OWN self?

Think not that there is any short cut to peace or harmony, save in correct living. Ye CANNOT go against thine own conscience and be at peace with thyself, thy home, thy neighbor, thy God! For as ye do it unto the least of thy brethren, ye do it unto thy Maker.

Ye have earned that right for much of this world's goods. Do not abuse that; else ye become — in thine OWN conscience — an outcast in this experience.   1901-1

35 Using Opportunities

Here is a time when forward movement is easily possible for all men. Because of this, one must be wary of outside influences, as these will have a greater strength than usual. Attention to one's duties, and the extension of one's spiritual path are the key to successful usage of this powerful time.

For remember, knowledge — or the seeking for the tree of knowledge — is the sin. It is the use of that you do know to the glory of God that is righteousness. 3633-1

It is not the knowledge, then, but what one does with one's abilities, one's opportunities in relationships to others, that makes for the development or retardment of that individual. 1293-1

. . . knowledge alone does not make one wise. With the abilities to use that thou hast in hand may there come understanding. 540-1

Changes come about . . . and some people term it "Lady Luck" or "The body is born under a lucky star." It's what the soul-mind has done *about* the source of redemption of the soul! 440-5

36 PERSEVERANCE

When circumstances prevent progress, even threatening one's ultimate continuation toward the goal, one does best to draw the light of his spiritual foundations within himself, to preserve it from harm. It is the warmth and constancy of this light which helps one to persevere in adversity, and to avoid the strong forces which attempt to turn him from his way.

. . . And do find patience with self. It has been said, "Have we not piped all the day long and no one has answered?" Seekest thou, as was given from this illustration, for the gratifying of thy self? Or seekest thou to be a channel of blessing to thy fellow man? They may not have answered as *thou* hast seen. They may have even shown contempt, as sneering, for thy patience and thy trouble. But *somewhere* the sun still shines; *somewhere* the day is done; for those that have grown weary, for those that have given up. The Lord abhorreth the quitter. And those temptations that come in such cases are the viewing of thine own *self*. Ye have hurt thyself and ye have again crucified thy Lord, when ye become impatient or speak harshly because someone has jeered or because someone has sneered or because someone has laughed at thy efforts!

Leave the *results*, leave the giving of the crown, leave the glory, with the Lord! *He* will repay! Thou sayest in thine own heart that thou believest. Then merely, simply, ACT that way! In speech, in thought, in deed. 518-2, A-1

37 Doing the Work

The creation of harmony depends upon each of those involved fulfilling his function, attending to his responsibilities. Words mean little unless they are supported by complementary action; then the words have reality and truth in them. Consistency in positive behavior is the greatest testimony to one's true merit.

As has been given of old, "Take that thou hast in hand." Use same day by day. And as that ye use, as that ye know is applied in those directions, those principles as indicated, in the home, in the daily labors, in the daily associations, social, material and otherwise, then that as is necessary for the next step is given.

And apply self in these directions — practical application! Not "I would like to do this, and when I am thus and so will I do this." For he that would save himself loseth all. For that ye give, *that ONLY* ye possess!   633-5

Then ask thyself the question — gain the answer first in thy physical consciousness: "What is my ideal of a SPIRITUAL life?" Then when the answer has come (for it has been given by Him that is Life) — that the kingdom of God — the kingdom of heaven — is within; and we view the kingdom of God without by the application of those things that are of the spirit of truth — these then answered, ye seek again in the inner consciousness: "Am I true to my ideal?"   987-4

38 friendship

As in 35, this is a time for inner strength, for preserving one's individuality although tempted to follow another path. Fellowship, friendship are positives, but they can be dangerous in that they may cause one to deviate from his way. In such matters one should move slowly, and with caution.

As to the associations with others, if ye would have friends, show thyself friendly. This does not mean becoming the butt of other's fun, nor of thy using others in the same manner. But if ye would have love, love others; do good to them, even that despitefully use you, even to those that misrepresent you. Not because it is ennobling, but because it is RIGHT in THY sight! Show thyself to be a son of the living Father, holy and acceptable unto Him; not ashamed, but keeping thy face towards the light and the shadows fall far behind.   1537-1

39 Reaffirmation

Any outward progress is ill-advised here. It is time for one to reaffirm contact with his spiritual source, to withdraw physically from the adverse outer conditions and give attention to his inner growth.

For whatever there may be is first conceived in spirit. It is acted upon by mind. Dependent, then, upon what the mind of the entity holds as its ideal, or as to what form or manner it would give by and through what spirit it would build in its mental self.

Hence the first injunction is to analyze self. What does the mind of this entity hold as its ideal in the spiritual world? What is the source of the entity's information? Is the author of thy faith, of thy belief, able to keep that ye commit unto it against any experience, be it spiritual, mental or material? Whoever is the author must himself have experienced spiritual, mental and material life. This must of itself, then, be the author of life; it must be the builder of mind as well as of material things. 2995-3

40 ƒORGIVENESS

Just as the sage harbors no resentment during a time of obstruction, so is he also forgiving of inferior behavior by those around him, when his freedom to progress is restored. It is by this tolerance, and by keeping the aspects of his life in proper proportion to his goal, that the sage succeeds.

If ye would be forgiven for that which is contrary to thy own purposes (yet through the vicissitudes of the experiences about thee, — anger and wrath give place to better judgment) — ye, too, will forgive those that have despitefully used thee — ye will hold no malice. For ye would that thy Ideal, that Way ye seek, hold no malice — yea, no judgment — against thee.

For this is the true law of recompense — yea — the true law of sacrifice.

For not in sacrifice alone has He sought His judgments, but rather in mercy, in grace, in fortitude — yea — in Divine love.

Hence as ye give, ye receive, For this is mercy, this is grace. This is the beauty of the inner life lived.   987-4

41 Controlling Reaction

Here the external world leans toward others, and one finds he is frustrated if he attempts anything on a large scale. The sage sees the tenor of the time and adheres to the peace of his spiritual source, thereby transcending any reaction to the adverse conditions. In this way one keeps the proper perspective and continues useful in helping others.

"If thy brother offend thee and smite thee on the right cheek, turn the other also."

This admonition becomes galling to many. But know that only in the same attitude, the same manner in which He met such rebuffs, such activities, may ye in thy satisfying, in thy bringing peace and harmony, find same in thine experience and thy relationships.

For remember, He is right in that given — "The soft answer turneth away wrath", and in that a gentleness, a kindness meted to those that have been and are in error but heapeth coals upon the mind, the heart, of those who have erred.

Then only in LOVING indifference may the conditions be met. What, ye say, is loving indifference? Acting as if it had not been, save disregarding — as if the conditions were NOT.

1402-2

42 applying the will

During a time of upswing, the
sage uses the burgeoning forces to improve
himself, purging the inferior aspects of his
personality, following the patterns of right
thinking. He knows that at such times it is
possible to achieve great progress, so he
chooses those directions which further good.

As we have indicated, there are two ways lying before the
entity. These may be chosen *best* by self; for the gift of the
Creative influence is that — in the life, or in material affairs,
termed in the lives of each soul — there are the abilities to
make self, through the application of will, one with the
constructive influences or to turn same to self's own in-
dulgencies.   352-1

See in self the virtues as well as the faults. Then magnify
the virtues, minimize the faults. Don't condemn self more than
you would be condemned by thy Maker.   5075-1

43 Resoluteness

The situation calls for honesty, within and without, and dedicated progress; resolute consistency, not force. The wise man, knowing the nature of the world, is ever mindful of his true position in the cosmos. He generously gives of himself and his resources in continuing his path.

The answers, then, are within thyself. For thy body is indeed the temple of the living God. There He has promised to meet thee, in the holy of holies — thy purpose, thy will.

Will ye make it then to be at one with His purpose? Let thy prayer ever be: LORD, HAVE THINE OWN WAY WITH ME. USE ME IN THE WAY AND MANNER THOU SEEST, O GOD, THAT I MAY BE THE GREATER CHANNEL OF BLESSINGS TO OTHERS, TO GLORIFY THEE — HERE AND NOW.

This is the attitude, my friend, that will bring thee closer and closer to the knowledge the understanding and — yea — with same the wisdom to apply that thou knowest.

He asketh not that ye apply that ye know not of, but desires that every soul "Seek and ye shall find, knock and it will be opened unto thee."

These are not merely sayings, beautiful to hear yet impractical in daily life! Have ye not observed and found that these are in keeping with the law? Like begets like. What ye sow ye reap. The Lord is one. To love mercy and to eschew evil is the duty of man. "If ye love me, ye will keep my commandments."   2524-3

44 ΛVOIDING EVIL

If one allows evil to become a part of his life, so that he is accustomed to its presence, he will fall under its power, eventually. Evil cannot survive the cosmic unity of the sage, who makes plain his intentions to continue on the path, and to eschew that which is less than beneficial to that end.

The answer is the application ever of will . . . Reckoning then as to whether will has ever been applied in more of the earth experiences, or has that of environmental used, rather than been used by, the entity itself. Get the point? Has the entity in its experience through its will *applied* that of will toward the development, or has it allowed itself to be used by the environment and become subject to environment, or has it developed itself through its will towards its own heredity position — for *all* are the children of God.   900-340

Again the cosmic forces swell positively, and progress on all levels is possible. Yet the sage, knowing how the scales tend to balance, is ever prepared for any turning of events. He holds his strong dedication to the path, and proceeds with inner constancy and outer sincerity.

. . . If the good man of the house knew when the thief was coming, he would be prepared. To be prepared would be to have the sword of the spirit, the purpose of the mind [ready].
2828-5

The application of will upon influences in the life alters the development of the inner man, the soul. Hold to that which is good, cleave to that which is right. Avoid even the appearance of evil. Thoughts are deeds and may become crimes or miracles. Never take advantage of your position or power, in order to exalt yourself, materially or mentally or in any way.   240-1

46 Building

It is through the consistency of his attention to his growth that the sage achieves cosmic unity. He uses every small action in an important way, for he knows that he thus develops the self toward perfection. This is a positive time, and one should progress confidently, maintaining a keen awareness of what he is building.

Remember ever that Mind in its entirety is ever the Builder. For it is step by step, line upon line, precept upon precept, here a little, there a little, that the attaining is accomplished in the mental, the spiritual, the material applications of an entity in this material world.   914-1

Be ye patient; be ye quiet and *see* the glory of the Lord in that thou may do in thine efforts day by day.   518-2

47 Right Perspective

 Conditions are lean, and the sage recognizes that the cycle has swung away from outward progress. He therefore waits quietly, keeping firm his inner self against the negative forces. He holds to his beliefs and manifests contentment and patience in the face of oppression.

To meet the disturbing factors with as much joyousness as if they were bringing pleasure in the material sight will alter much in the heart and mind of the seeker. For that which is, is a result of the thinking of individuals as related one to another.   610-1

Count thy hardships, thy troubles, even thy disappointments rather as stepping-stones to know His way better.   262-83

Remember the sources, as we have indicated, are the meeting of one's own self; this is karmic. It can be met most in Him who, taking away the law of cause and effect by fulfilling the law, established the law of grace. Thus the entity needs to lean upon the arm of Him who is the law, and the truth and the light.   2828-4

48 Understanding Change

Here is a difficult time, in need of spiritual stability, beset by the uncertainties of transformation. In such an environment of change, it is the responsibility of one who possesses a constant reservoir of inner strength to provide encouragement to others, and to influence them toward helping each other.

. . . All that thou may accomplish of a material nature changes and fades day by day. But that thou hast sown, that thou has given in the fruits of the spirit . . . grows and becomes a part of thine own soul self-development.   270-36, A-24

Oft is He disappointed in thee, but if thou dost bring such into the minds, the hearts, the lives of others, what is thy reflection but these same experiences?

But to love good, to flee from evil, to bring the awareness of the God-Consciousness, into the minds and hearts of others, is THY purpose in this experience.   826-11

There is a proper timing for every action, and the success of the action hangs on that timing. Change is most often a gradual progression, not a sudden upheaval. One should note the manner in which the seasons progress, and patiently build toward the desired transformation. Achieved in this way, the change occurs naturally, and gains support from others.

COMMENCE with the associations first in those lines that are in keeping with abilities of the body, by its own initiative, its own purposes, its own desires.

And this, as development, is as a first law. Do first things first, and then — as there is the understanding the application comes; and day by day it grows not only in import but in purpose and in activity.

DO NOT let the vastness or the shadow of what may be the outcome topple the basis or the purposes; for if the basic principles are the correct ones in the foundation, no matter to what heights nor to what extent nor in what great scope of activity it may advance, basic principles being first correct, it would not be over heavy.   165-24

But make haste SLOWLY! Prepare the body. Prepare the mind, before ye attempt to loosen it in such measures or manners that it may be taken hold upon by those influences which constantly seek expressions of self rather than of a living, constructive influence of a CRUCIFIED Savior.   2475-1

50 keeping the way

A propitious time, conducive to achievement. Yet, if one is careless about the rightness of one's action, disaster can result. It may be that the task is too great for one's strength, or that adequate preparation has not been made. Before using the positive external forces, one must be certain that the internal self is ready emotionally and in line spiritually.

Be upright, straightforward, doing the duty ever; relying on the Right to carry through. 487-29, A-15

The withered rod became the budded almond in the hands of him who sought to know His ways, and applied same in his life. Keep thine eyes, thine heart, ever to that source from which emanates all power that lifts man toward the Creator. 39-3

For all life is one, all force is one, and when one applies self and attains through attunement, through that consciousness that may approach the universal consciousness, then those experiences sought may come through. 136-78, A-1

When a sudden change of events brings upheaval into the life of the sage, his reaction is to examine himself and his actions, lest he behave in a faithless way. It is the internal self that is at stake, and one must learn to remain calm in the face of the apparent disasters of this world if that self is ever to transcend materiality.

Q. How can I keep from worrying?
A. Why worry, when ye may pray?
Know that the power of thyself is very limited. The power of Creative Forces is unlimited.   2981-1

In an hour of trial, when there are influences abroad that would change or mar, or take away that freedom which is the gift of the Creative Forces to man; that man might by his own innate desire be at-one with God, the Father as was manifested in Jesus, the Christ; there should be the willingness to pattern the life, the emergencies, the exigencies as may arise, much in the way and manner as the Master indicated to each and every soul.   602-7

52 focusing

Attaining inner calm is basic to the achievements of cosmic unity. To attain this state one must develop control over the body and mind, so as to be able to focus the direction of the self to the immediate situation. This is a time for withdrawing, for concentrating on the internal harmony.

Thy purposes then, thy heart and thy life must be a consistent thing! For if thine eye be single (the I Am, that is, — the purposes, the desires — and ye work at it) then thy WHOLE BODY is full of light. 1537-1

And those influences in the emotions — unless they are governed by an ideal — may often become a stumbling-stone! 1599-1

. . . Work where you are. As was given to those who were called, "The ground upon which ye stand is holy." Begin where you are. 4021-1

53 GROWTH

Conditions bode well, but there is the need for patience, for allowing things to progress as they should. This is no time to attempt to force issues. Growth is a gradual process, and one must learn that only by the practice of consistent virtue can he become the sage of his ideals.

Truth is growth! For what is truth today may be tomorrow only partially so, to a developing soul! 1297-1

But truth is a growing thing, as infinity, as Creative Force. For it is a constant growth. Only good lives . . .

As life itself is one, so is the work one. The work in the present is a growing or a preparation for the next step. For ye are indeed gods in the growth. And as we apply today, tomorrow's step is given us. . . 1554-6

54 hinðrances

Here one finds himself in a position where assertive behavior brings ruin, and where one lacks the position he feels deserving of. The sage, through his understanding and cosmic perspective, overcomes any self-pity. He keeps his internal focus on the ultimate goal of spiritual fullness and transcends the apparently negative condition.

So let not those things which may not in the present be understood weary thy soul, but know that some time, somewhere, you, too, will understand. Keep the faith.   5369-2

When opportunities are presented, it is the entity's own will force that must be exercised. . . Then in every contact with others, there is the opportunity for a soul to fulfill or meet in itself the Creative Forces from the First Cause, and to embrace that which is necessary for the entity to enter into at-oneness with the Creative Force. Hence the entity is ever on the road.
903-23

55 purposefulness

When conditions, as here, have reached the optimum, the sage knows the cycle must turn. However, he utilizes the cosmic fullness while it is with him, rendering positive decisions concerning his fellows, shedding the clear light of truth on all within his reach.

Keep the mental attitude towards constructive forces ever. Be not only worthwhile but worthwhile for something. Purposeful and constructive in all its [one's] activities is what should ever be; and this naturally keeps the attitude — with creating a balance in the body — near to the proper coordinating forces.

1005-17

Do that thou *knowest* to do, TODAY! Then leave the results, leave the rewards, leave the effects into the hands of thy God. For *He* knoweth thy heart, and He hath called — if ye will harken.

518-2

56 transition

Conditions are unstable and transitory, requiring the utmost caution. The emphasis is on movement, and on one's consistent attention to propriety while caught in this flux. Any decision must be carefully made, and assertiveness is not called for. Small things, germane to the goal, may be done successfully.

Each cycle brings a soul-entity to another crossroad, or another urge from one or several of its activities in the material plane.

But these are chosen with the purpose to indicate to the entity how and why those urges are a part of the entity's experience as a unit, or as a whole.

For one enters a material sojourn not by chance, but there is brought into being the continuity of pattern or purposes, and each soul is attracted to those influences that may be visioned from above. Thus THERE the turns in the river of life may be viewed.

To be sure, there are floods in the life, there are dark days and there are days of sunshine. But the soul-entity stayed in a purpose that is creative may find the haven of peace as is declared in Him.   3128-1

57 Gentle Progress

The conditions require skillful handling, since progress is called for, and is possible if properly executed. One should make his intentions known, so that others may think them through. This will enhance the possibilities of cooperation. Then one should proceed, gradually, but with a penetrating firmness, toward the goal. Care must be taken not to be too assertive (nor too weak) and to not persist when it is time to cease. This is a difficult time, and one should maintain a spiritual awareness, to assist and guide him.

Be thou strong in the purposes of thy life. Ye are in the material plane, yea — but unless the house that ye build is founded upon the spirit of truth it is as the house builded upon the sand. Then, fortify thyself in being oft in prayer, of coming close to the loving arms of thy Savior and of thy God. For he that oft draws nigh will not wander far afield . . .

Keep the faith. Walk in the light. Let no darkness be in thee at all. For *He* is the light, the truth and the way, and He is willing — if thou wilt but walk with Him.

As the ways come and go in thine experience that bring to thee the understanding as to the meeting and applying of those things pertaining to the material life, so is there the growth in the spiritual life that gives the purposefulness in all the activities in a material experience. . .   792-1

58 Contentment

Even in a time of joy, one must remain inwardly strong, aware of the direction of his thoughts. It is so easy to relax, to let oneself flow contentedly with pleasure. If pleasure's route is away from the path, one may be swept along with it. It is better to integrate this positive force into the fellowship of one's life in a manner that benefits both one's outward and inward growth.

Turn then to those things within. Know the law and then apply it daily. Not by some great thing. Smile often. Speak gently. Speak kindly. Go out of the way to do a kind deed, and ye will find that He will walk closer with thee, and thy life, thy purpose will become a glorious thing in this experience.

3376-2

In the application then in the present in these fields of activity should the entity find that channel for not only the greater expression of self that has been gained through its sojourns in the earth, but the greater contentment in that which will make for — in contentment — a growth. While storms and trials are necessary in every soul, as we see manifested in nature, only in contentment does *growth* make manifest. Not contentment to that point of satisfaction, for a satisfied mind or soul ceases to seek. But only in contentment may it receive and give out. In *giving* does a soul grow, even as a tree, even as a rock, even as a sunset, even as a world *grows* in its influence upon that about it. . .

699-1

59 Purification

The wise man knows that often it is only through separating himself from the apparent flow of his worldly life that true growth can begin. There are also aspects of the self which must be dissolved before progress can be made. The sage is one who dissipates his ego through dedication of his life to a spiritual goal.

Study to show thyself approved unto God, rightly divining the words of truth, keeping self unspotted from the world. Though the world hate thee, be not *of* the world. Though things, conditions, appearances, may grow as to be red, dark, black — if thine heart, thine soul is founded in Him, the *dawn* shall come!
792-1

First, the entering of *every* soul is that it, the soul, may become more and more aware or conscious of the divine within, that the soul-body may be purged that it may be a fit companion for the *glory* of the Creative Forces in its activity.

Then again, in the appearances, do not look or seek for the phenomenon of the experience without the purpose, the aim. *Use* same as a criterion, as what to do and what not to do. Not that it, the simple experience, has made or set *any*thing permanent! For there is the constant change evidenced before us; until the soul has been washed clean through that the soul in its body, in its temple, has *experienced* by the manner in which it has acted, has spoken, has thought, has desired in its relationships to its fellow man!
518-2

60 Limitation

Restrictions on conduct are necessary in our world, but it is important to achieve a balance even in the area of restrictions. Too little or too great limitation is unsatisfacotry. To be able to determine what is proper, the sage creates a personal code of ethics, which has its roots in his idealism. Once he has this means of measurement, he can define the boundaries of his behavior in a manner which guides but does not frustrate.

As has been indicated, a little more patient, a little more tolerant, a little more humble. But not a tolerance that becomes timid, — this would make rebellion in self. Not a patience that is not positive. Not humbleness that becomes morbid or lacking in beauty. For as orderliness is a part of thy being, so let consistency — as persistency — be a part of thy being.   1402-1

61 Sympathy

When one must deal with difficult people, he should concentrate on being internally firm and externally gentle. In this way he can manifest the penetrating understanding necessary for fruitful communication. Through discussion and sympathy, the sage gains knowledge needed in making a truly just decision, thereby averting disharmony.

All knowledge is to be used in the manner that will give help and assistance to others, and the desire is that the laws of the Creator be manifested in the physical world. For as given, be faithful and subdue the world. All power is given through knowledge and understanding.　　　　254-17

And in thy dealings with thy brother, meet rather that as would be if conditions were reversed; being patient, being understanding; not as preachments but rather as following of precepts and living the ideal that is manifest in the word of the entity.　　　　2524-4

62 humility

Here is a time for modesty and honest humility. Assertive behavior meets with grief. At such times the sage manifests simplicity in his behavior, adhering to the central view, exhibiting sincerity and reverence. In this way, he is not diverted from his path by this difficult period.

To continue to condemn only brings condemnation, then, for self. This does not mean that self's activity should be passive, but rather being constant in prayer — knowing and taking — knowing and understanding that he that is faithful is not given a burden beyond that he is able to bear, — if he will put the burden upon Him that has given the promise, "I will be with thee; there shall not come that which shall harm thee, if thou will but put thy trust, thy faith in me."

Know that only in Him, who may bring peace and harmony by or through the contacts — the thoughts of self in relationship to the whole — may there be brought better relationships.

First make an analysis of self, of self's relationships, of the impelling influences that cause others to act in their manners in the present.

Do not condemn self; do not condemn another, but leave the activities that would bring about condemnation rather in His hands — who requireth at the hands of all — that there be meted, "As ye would that others do to thee, do ye even so to thy fellow man!" 290-1

63 Using Caution

A consistent and well-prepared progression is called for here. Overconfidence, stemming from a good beginning, invites disaster. Conditions are precipitous, requiring slow and cautious movement. Although progress is possible, one must be ever-receptive to any change in the cosmic winds, or all that has been gained may be lost.

For an entity should comprehend and KNOW and NEVER forget, that life and its experiences are only what one puts into same! And unless the activities, the thoughts are CONTINUOUSLY constructive, and the experience well-balanced, the entity CANNOT, WILL not fulfill the purpose for which it came into the present experience.

Do not engage in those things in which question marks are set, not only for thyself but for thy children, for thy Lord.

Study to show thyself approved unto Him, a workman not ashamed; rightly divining the words of truth and keeping self UNSPOTTED from thine own conscience that so oft berates thee — or keeping thyself unspotted from the world.   1537-1

64 Completion

The wise man knows that every moment is as critical as any other to the success of the journey. When the time of completion nears, he does not allow his dedication to flag, but maintains his spiritually-deliberate progress. He separates things carefully, weighing their importance relative to the goal, before he acts. It is this consistent thoroughness that carries him onward.

An individual entity's experience must be finished before the entity may either be blotted out or come into full brotherhood with the greater abilities, or the greater applications of self in the creating or finishing of that begun.

Each appearance in the earth is an opportunity given thee by the grace of God. The fact of being aware of thyself is assurance of the fact that the Father-God is mindful of thee, NOW, TODAY.

Each soul enters with a mission. And even as Jesus, the great missionary, we all have a mission to perform. Are we working with Him [continually], or just now and then? Seek, then, His way, for He changeth not.   3003-1

Nothing prevents [soul or spiritual development], only self.

Keep the shadow of self away. Turn thy face to the light and the shadows fall behind.   987-4

upper / lower	☰	☳	☵	☶	☷	☴	☲	☱
☰	1	34	5	26	11	9	14	43
☳	25	51	3	27	24	42	21	17
☵	6	40	29	4	7	59	64	47
☶	33	62	39	52	15	53	56	31
☷	12	16	8	23	2	20	35	45
☴	44	32	48	18	46	57	50	28
☲	13	55	63	22	36	37	30	49
☱	10	54	60	41	19	61	38	58

THE EDGAR CAYCE LEGACIES

Among the vast resources which have grown out of the late Edgar Cayce's work are:

The Readings: Available for examination and study at the Association for Research and Enlightenment, Inc., (A.R.E.) at Virginia Beach, Va. are 14,256 readings consisting of 49,135 pages of verbatim psychic material plus related correspondence. *The readings* are the clairvoyant discourses given by Cayce while he was in a self-induced hypnotic sleep-state. These discourses were recorded in shorthand and then typed. Copious indexing and cross-indexing make the readings readily accessible for study.

Research and Information: Medical information which flowed through Cayce is being researched and applied by the research divisions of the Edgar Cayce Foundation. Work is also being done with dreams and other aspects of ESP. Much information is disseminated through the A.R.E. Press publications, *A.R.E. News* and *The A.R.E. Journal.* Co-ordination of a nation-wide program of lectures and conferences is in the hands of the Department of Education. A library specializing in psychic literature is available to the public with books on loan to members. An extensive tape library has A.R.E. lectures available for purchase or loan to members. Resource material has been made available for authors, resulting in the publication of scores of books, booklets and other material.

A.R.E. Study Groups: The Edgar Cayce material is most valuable when worked with in an A.R.E. Study Group, the text for which is *A Search for God,* Books I and II. These books are the outcome of eleven years of work by Edgar Cayce with the first A.R.E. group and represent the distillation of wisdom which flowed through him in the trance condition. Hundreds of A.R.E. groups flourish throughout the United States and other countries. Their primary purpose is to assist the members to know their relationship to their Creator and to become channels of love and service to others. The groups are nondenominational and avoid ritual and dogma. There are no dues or fees required to join a group although contributions may be accepted.

Membership: A.R.E. has an open-membership policy which offers attractive benefits.

For more information write A.R.E., Box 595, Virginia Beach, Va. 23451. To obtain information about publications, please direct your query to A.R.E. Press. To obtain information about joining or perhaps starting an A.R.E. Study Group, please direct your letter to the Study Group Department.